The Infinite Metaverse:

The Next Frontier of Technology and Humanity

By James S. Goble

Table of Contents

Introduction

The phrase "metaverse" refers to a group of virtual worlds, online games, social networks, and digital platforms that allow individuals to engage with each other and with digital information in immersive and realistic ways. The term "metaverse" was popularized by Neal Stephenson's science fiction book Snow Crash, which alluded to a large, shared, and permanent virtual environment that included the whole spectrum of human experience. Since then, the metaverse has progressed from a fictitious concept to a real and developing reality that is changing the way we interact, work, play, learn, and create.

The metaverse is a network of linked and interoperable virtual places that span many devices, apps, and media, rather than a single location or platform. The metaverse, like the real world, is not a static or permanent environment, but rather one that is molded by the activities and preferences of its users, producers, and developers. The metaverse is a live, breathing digital environment with limitless opportunities for exploration, expression, and creation.

The goal of this book is to look at present and future metaverse developments and how they will affect technology, society, and mankind. The book will look at the metaverse's history and growth, the essential traits and qualities that characterize it, the primary difficulties and possibilities it brings, and the best practices and tactics for navigating and thriving in it. The book will also examine how some of the most visible and important instances of the metaverse, including Fortnite, Roblox, Minecraft, Decentraland, and Facebook Horizon, are altering the culture and economics of the digital era.

Anyone interested in learning more about the metaverse, whether they are casual users, enthusiastic gamers, content producers, entrepreneurs, educators, academics, or policymakers, should read this book. The book's goal is to present a thorough and approachable explanation of the metaverse, as well as a critical and forward-thinking viewpoint on its implications and promise. The book's goal is to excite and enlighten readers about the metaverse, as well as to urge them to participate in and contribute to this fascinating and transformational digital frontier.

Chapter One: The Metaverse's Development and Evolution

The phrase "metaverse" refers to a shared virtual reality in which individuals may interact, create, and explore in a variety of ways. Science fiction literature, movies, and games such as Ready Player One, The Matrix, and Fortnite have popularized the notion of the metaverse. The metaverse, on the other hand, is a genuine potential that is being formed by technology and societal developments. In this part, we will look at the four major trends driving the metaverse's growth and evolution:

Immersive technology convergence: Immersive technologies such as virtual reality (VR), augmented reality (AR), mixed reality (MR), and spatial computing allow users to interact with and alter digital material in increasingly realistic and engaging ways. Because of advancements in hardware, software, and cloud computing, these technologies are becoming more accessible, economical, and powerful.

For example, Facebook's Oculus Quest 2 standalone VR headset costs $299 and has high-quality visuals, wireless networking, and hand tracking. For $3,500, Microsoft's HoloLens 2 MR headset projects holograms into the real world and enables users to interact with them via gestures and voice commands. These technologies are paving the way for the metaverse to become a more immersive and pervasive platform for entertainment, education, communication, and productivity.

Online communities and social networks are expanding:

Online communities and social networks provide venues for users to interact, communicate, and cooperate with people who share the same interests, beliefs, or objectives. Because of the development of digital devices, the expansion of internet access, and the rise of new kinds of media and expression, these platforms are becoming more varied, inclusive, and influential. Discord, for example, is a platform with over 150 million monthly active users that lets users establish and join chat servers for a variety of themes such as gaming, music, art, and education. TikTok is a platform with over 1 billion monthly active users that lets users make and share short movies with music, filters, and effects. These platforms are paving the way for the metaverse to become a more varied and lively platform by providing additional options for social engagement, content production, and cultural exchange.

The Rise of Digital Ecosystems and Economies:

Users may produce, trade, and consume digital products and services such as games, applications, music, films, and art in digital economies and ecosystems. Because of the adoption of new business models, the integration of new technology, and the engagement of new stakeholders, these systems are becoming more dynamic, inventive, and useful. Roblox, for example, is a game-creation-and-playing platform with over 40 million daily active players and over 8 million creators. Non-fungible tokens (NFTs) are digital assets that represent unique and rare digital things, such as art, music, and collectibles, and may be validated and exchanged on blockchain networks like Ethereum. These technologies are paving the way for the metaverse to become a more dynamic and inventive platform by opening up new avenues for economic activity, creative expression, and value generation.

The emergence of ethical and regulatory issues:
Privacy, security, identification, ownership, governance, and inclusion are examples of ethical and regulatory difficulties that emerge as a result of the creation and usage of the metaverse. As the metaverse gets more immersive, widespread, and influential, these challenges become more complicated, serious, and contentious. Horizon, Facebook's

metaverse project, is a virtual reality social platform that enables users to build and explore virtual worlds, but it also raises concerns about how Facebook will gather, use, and share user data, as well as how it would govern user behavior and content. The planned EU Digital Services Act and Digital Markets Act seek to promote a fair and secure digital environment for consumers and companies, but they also pose obstacles to the metaverse's creativity and competitiveness. These challenges need careful analysis, cooperation, and regulation, and they are helping to shape the metaverse into a more ethical and responsible platform.

These four tendencies are not mutually exclusive, but rather interconnected and interdependent, and they are determining the metaverse's future. The metaverse is a network of platforms linked by common standards, protocols, and interfaces, rather than a single platform. The metaverse is a dynamic process that is always changing and extending, rather than a static state. The metaverse is a contemporary reality that is already changing the way we live, work, study, and play.

The Perspective for the Metaverse to Support Social Causes and Activism

With its large and diversified user base, the metaverse has the potential to be a significant instrument for social concerns and action. The metaverse might help social causes by increasing awareness and finances for topics like climate change, human rights, and healthcare. Users have organized virtual fundraising events for organizations such as the American Cancer Society and Doctors Without Borders in virtual environments such as Second Life. These events may draw enormous crowds and generate considerable sums of money for a good cause.

Furthermore, the metaverse might serve as a haven for political criticism and action. Online activism and dissent are highly watched and controlled in many countries, making it difficult for activists to express their ideas and organize without fear of retaliation. Because of its decentralized and pseudonymous character, the metaverse might offer a safe venue for people to vent their dissatisfaction and organize demonstrations. This may be especially significant in nations with harsh governments or restricted freedom of speech.

Furthermore, the metaverse might serve as a venue for disadvantaged people to organize and argue for their rights. LGBTQ+ communities, disability rights organizations, and other social justice movements have already emerged in virtual worlds such as Second Life and World of Warcraft. Individuals may interact with others who have had similar experiences and fight for their rights in a secure and supportive setting in these virtual worlds.

Overall, the metaverse has considerable potential to help social concerns and activism. The metaverse might assist to magnify the voices of oppressed people and create genuine change in the real world by offering a venue for raising awareness, fundraising, and political protest.

Chapter Two: Metaverse Scenarios and Outcomes in the Next Ten Years

The metaverse is a network of linked virtual worlds that provide a variety of experiences and possibilities, rather than a single platform or technology. The following are some of the metaverse's primary features:

- It is persistent, which means that it persists indefinitely and is not dependent on the presence or activities of any specific user.

- It is synchronous, which means it enables real-time communication and cooperation among users on various platforms and devices.

- It is immersive, which means that it gives a high-fidelity and accurate reproduction of the physical world, as well as innovative and creative surroundings that transcend reality's constraints.

- It is inclusive, which means that it is available to and inexpensive to anybody, regardless of geography, identity, or background.

- It is open, which means it is built on interoperable standards and protocols that allow users to travel freely and fluidly across virtual worlds, as well as produce and control their content and assets.

The metaverse is still in its early phases, and many uncertainties and obstacles must be solved before it can become a mainstream phenomenon. Some of the important elements influencing the metaverse's future are:

- The development and use of technology and software that allow immersive and interactive virtual experiences, such as VR/AR headsets, haptic devices, cloud computing, 5G, blockchain, and artificial intelligence.

- Privacy, security, trust, identity, ownership, governance, ethics, and diversity are examples of social and cultural norms and values that impact the expectations and actions of metaverse users and producers.

- Monetization, taxes, regulation, competition, and cooperation are examples of economic and commercial strategies and incentives that drive the expansion and sustainability of the metaverse.

Based on these considerations, we may picture three different metaverse situations and results during the next ten years:

- The ideal scenario: In this scenario, the metaverse is a thriving and diversified ecosystem in which users and creators may express themselves, engage with others, and follow their hobbies and interests. The metaverse is widely available and inexpensive, and it provides a range of high-quality and engaging experiences that improve users' well-being and productivity. As it supports education, creativity, inclusivity, and activism, the metaverse is also a platform for social good and constructive change. The metaverse is controlled by a democratic and transparent system that protects and promotes the rights and interests of all stakeholders while encouraging cooperation and interoperability across various platforms and communities.

- The dystopian scenario: The metaverse is a fragmented and unfriendly environment in which users and creators are exploited for the advantage of a few strong and dominating organizations. The metaverse is exclusive and pricey, with a restricted and low-quality selection of experiences designed to divert and deceive consumers. As it magnifies disinformation, violence, bigotry, and addiction, the metaverse is also a platform for societal damage and bad influence. The metaverse is managed by an authoritarian and opaque system that violates the rights and interests of the vast majority of stakeholders while imposing isolation and lock-in across various platforms and communities.

- The realistic scenario: In this scenario, the metaverse is a heterogeneous and dynamic ecosystem that provides users and producers with both possibilities and problems. To some degree, the metaverse is accessible and inexpensive, and it provides diversified and somewhat high-quality experiences that gratify and impact consumers.

As it facilitates education, innovation, inclusiveness, and activism, as well as disinformation, violence, prejudice, and addiction, the metaverse is a platform for both social good and social evil. The metaverse is controlled by a hybrid and complicated system that balances the rights and interests of many stakeholders while also allowing for some degree of cooperation and interoperability across various platforms and communities.

Chapter Three: How to Apply Metaverse Trends to Various Domains, Industries, and Contexts

The metaverse is a network of linked digital environments that span the physical, virtual, and augmented worlds, rather than a single platform or technology. The metaverse is projected to have a significant influence on a variety of areas, industries, and settings, including:

- Education: Immersive simulations, virtual field excursions, collaborative projects, and individualized feedback are some of the new chances for learning and teaching that the metaverse may provide. The metaverse may also provide learners from all backgrounds, places, and abilities with access to high-quality education, as well as promote lifelong learning and skill development.

- Entertainment: New types of entertainment and narrative, including interactive games, social experiences, live events, and user-generated material, may be found in the metaverse. The metaverse may also enable content providers, developers, and platforms to build new business models and income streams, as well as empower users to express their creativity and identity.

- Commerce: The metaverse has the potential to revolutionize the way individuals purchase and sell products and services such as virtual items, digital assets, experiences, and knowledge.

Additionally, the metaverse may allow new kinds of value generation and exchange, such as peer-to-peer transactions, tokenization, and blockchain-based systems, as well as improve consumer engagement and loyalty.

- Healthcare: Telemedicine, remote monitoring, diagnosis, and treatment, as well as mental health and wellbeing, are examples of how the metaverse might enhance the quality and accessibility of healthcare. The metaverse may also support novel healthcare applications such as virtual reality treatment, biofeedback, and gamification, as well as health education and prevention.

- Social: The metaverse may improve people's ability to interact and engage with others, such as friends, family, coworkers, and communities. The metaverse may also enhance social inclusion and diversity by enabling new types of social engagement and cooperation, such as avatars, virtual places, and shared experiences.

Some ways for applying metaverse trends to various disciplines, industries, and situations include:

> ➤ Identify the needs and opportunities: The first stage is to identify the target domain's, sector's, or context's existing and future requirements and opportunities, as well as the problems and hurdles that may impede metaverse adoption. This may be accomplished via market research, user study, stakeholder analysis, and exploration of

current and upcoming metaverse platforms and technologies.

> Design the solutions and experiences: The next phase is to create solutions and experiences that meet the demands and opportunities of the target domain, sector, or context, as well as the users' and customers' expectations and preferences. This may be accomplished via the use of human-centered design approaches like empathy, ideation, prototyping, and testing, as well as by using the metaverse's unique

characteristics and capabilities such as immersion, interaction, and interoperability.

> execute and assess the results: The last phase is to execute and analyze the outcomes of the solutions and experiences built for the target domain, sector, or context, as well as the effect and value that they have produced for users and customers. This may be accomplished via the use of agile and iterative approaches such as scrum, sprints, and feedback loops, as well as by the measurement and analysis of key

performance indicators such as user pleasure, engagement, retention, and revenue.

Chapter Four: The Metaverse's Future

The phrase "metaverse" refers to a shared virtual reality in which individuals may interact, produce, and consume digital information. It is a network of linked virtual worlds that provide different and engaging experiences, rather than a single platform or technology. The metaverse is a fast-evolving reality with the potential to revolutionize numerous parts of our society, economics, and culture.

We examined the present status and potential prospects of the metaverse in this book, concentrating on four main dimensions: technology, content, business, and social. We investigated how technology developments such as cloud computing, 5G, blockchain, artificial intelligence, and augmented and virtual reality allow the metaverse. We've also spoken about how the development and consumption of many sorts of digital material, such as gaming, entertainment, education, art, and social media, influence the metaverse.

Furthermore, we examined how the business models and tactics of various stakeholders, such as platform providers, content producers, advertising, and consumers, affect the metaverse. Finally, we looked at how the metaverse affects social and ethical elements of our lives, such as identity, privacy, security, governance, and inclusion.

This book's primary discoveries and ideas may be summarized as follows:

- The metaverse is a complex and dynamic entity that evolves and expands in several directions and dimensions. It is a diverse and flexible idea that represents the variety and inventiveness of its participants and producers, rather than a monolithic or static one.

- The metaverse is a collaborative and interactive arena in which people are empowered and engaged. It is not a passive or isolated environment, but one that encourages engagement and co-creation among its members and communities.
- The metaverse is a revolutionary and disruptive force that challenges and disrupts the status quo of numerous businesses and sectors. It is a dramatic and paradigmatic innovation that provides new possibilities and risks for current and rising actors and markets,

rather than a complementary or incremental one. The metaverse is an intriguing and hopeful idea that inspires and encourages its supporters. It is neither a dystopian or utopian future, but rather one that demands vision and action from its stakeholders and supporters.

The Most Important Takeaways and Lessons

The following are the important insights and lessons learned from this book:

- The metaverse is a dynamic and emergent process that is defined by the decisions and actions of its participants and producers, rather than a set or planned conclusion. As a result, it is critical to be aware of and educated about the metaverse's recent trends and developments, as well as to be proactive and participate in influencing its future direction and growth.

- The metaverse is not a distinct or isolated domain, but rather one that is linked and interconnected with other domains of our society, economics, and culture. As a result, it is critical to analyze and handle the metaverse's larger implications and ramifications, as well as to balance and align its advantages and hazards for various stakeholders and interests.

- The metaverse is a complicated and demanding enterprise that requires cooperation and coordination among numerous players and entities. As a result, it is critical to build and maintain effective and efficient procedures and frameworks for metaverse governance and regulation, as well as to nurture and promote ethical and responsible metaverse activities and behaviors.

We hope that this book has given you a thorough and informative understanding of the metaverse, as well as a helpful and inspirational roadmap for your future participation and interaction with it. We feel that the metaverse is not just a fascinating concept, but also one that has the potential to improve and enhance our lives in a variety of ways. We encourage you to join us on the adventure of finding and building the metaverse and to share your views and opinions with us and the larger metaverse community. Thank you for taking the time to read this book, and we hope to see you in the metaverse!